BAOFENG RADIO USER GUIDE FOR BEGINNERS

A COMPLETE MASTERY GUIDE TO LEARN HOW TO PROFESSIONALLY USE THE BAOFENG RADIO, AND UNLOCK THE POWER OF COMMUNICATION EVEN AS A BEGINNER

HERRICK DAKOTA

Copyright Notice

TABLE OF CONTENTS

BAOFENG RADIO USER GUIDE

Introduction:

Welcome to the Baofeng Radio User's Guide: Mastering Your Communication. In a world where connectivity is key, the Baofeng radio stands as a beacon of versatile communication. As the author of this guide, I am thrilled to be your companion on this journey, unraveling the secrets of a device that transcends mere communication—it's a gateway to seamless interaction, whether in the great outdoors, during emergencies, or in professional settings.

Join me in exploring the multifaceted universe of Baofeng radios. This guide is more than a manual; it's a roadmap to empower you, whether you're a beginner navigating the waves for the first time or an experienced user seeking to unlock advanced functionalities. From the nuanced details of the display panel to the intricacies of programming channels, each chapter is crafted to elevate your understanding and proficiency.

Baofeng radios have etched their place as a stalwart in the realm of two-way communication. In this guide, we'll uncover the reasons behind their popularity and showcase how these devices transcend the ordinary, providing a canvas for effective communication in various scenarios.

This guide is not just about button presses and frequencies; it's a passport to mastering the art of communication. From the basics of setting up your radio to advanced features and real-world applications, each section is designed to empower you with the knowledge needed to make the most of your Baofeng device.

Get ready to embark on a journey where communication knows no bounds. Whether you're an enthusiast, an adventurer, or a professional, the Baofeng Radio User's Guide is your compass in the world of wireless communication. Let's dive in and master the waves together.

Chapter 1

Overview of Baofeng Radio

In the dynamic landscape of two-way radios, Baofeng has emerged as a trailblazer, seamlessly blending innovation with reliability. This overview serves as your gateway to understanding the essence of Baofeng, from its inception to its unparalleled impact on communication landscapes.

The Baofeng saga begins with a commitment to democratizing communication. Originating in China, Baofeng Communication Equipment Co. Ltd. was founded in 2001. With a vision to make high-quality, feature-rich radios accessible to all, Baofeng has since evolved into a global leader. Explore the milestones that mark this journey, from the introduction of their first handheld transceiver to the continuous refinement of cutting-edge radio technology.

Baofeng radios aren't just devices; they are enablers of connectivity in diverse settings. From outdoor enthusiasts relishing adventures to emergency responders navigating critical situations, Baofeng radios play a vital role. Uncover the significance of these radios in fostering effective communication, bridging distances, and ensuring seamless coordination in various scenarios.

Common Terms For Baofeng Radio Operations

1. **Frequency:**

The rate at which a radio signal oscillates, measured in Hertz (Hz), kilohertz (kHz), megahertz (MHz), or gigahertz (GHz).

- Example: The FM radio band operates in the frequency range of 88 MHz to 108 MHz.

2. **Channel:**

A predetermined frequency or combination of frequencies used for communication between radios.

- Example: Channel 1 may be programmed to transmit and receive on a frequency of 462.5625 MHz.

3. **Squelch**:

A circuit that mutes the audio output of a radio when no signal is present, preventing background noise from being heard.

- Example: Adjusting the squelch level on a Baofeng radio eliminates static noise when no incoming signal is detected.

4. **CTCSS (Continuous Tone-Coded Squelch System):**

A method of filtering out unwanted radio transmissions by using sub-audible tones to selectively open the squelch only for signals with the correct tone.

- Example: Baofeng radios can be programmed with specific CTCSS tones to access or filter out transmissions on designated channels.

5. **DCS (Digital-Coded Squelch):**

A digital squelch system that uses encoded digital signals to selectively open the squelch on compatible radios.

- Example: Baofeng radios equipped with DCS capabilities can communicate with other radios using compatible DCS codes for added privacy and security.

6. **VOX (Voice-Operated Transmission):**

A feature that enables hands-free operation of a radio by automatically transmitting when the user speaks into the microphone.

- Example: Baofeng radios with VOX functionality allow users to activate transmission by voice command without pressing the Push-To-Talk (PTT) button.

7. **PTT (Push-To-Talk):**

A button or switch on a radio that, when pressed, activates transmission and allows the user to speak into the microphone.

- Example: Pressing the PTT button on a Baofeng radio initiates transmission, allowing the user to communicate with other radios on the same channel.

8. **Repeater:**

A radio station that receives signals on one frequency and retransmits them on another frequency to extend the range of communication.

- Example: Baofeng radios can access repeaters to communicate over longer distances or in areas with obstructed line-of-sight.

9. **Scan**:

A function that automatically searches and monitors multiple channels or frequencies for activity, allowing users to listen for incoming transmissions.

- Example: Baofeng radios can be set to scan a range of frequencies to detect and monitor active channels.

10. **Programming:**

The process of configuring a radio's settings, channels, frequencies, and features using programming software or manual input.

- Example: Programming a Baofeng radio involves entering desired frequencies, assigning channels, setting squelch levels, and configuring other parameters for optimal performance.

Chapter Two
Getting Started With Your Baofeng Radio

Unboxing And Checking Your Radio

Carefully unpack and check the transceiver to confirm that the items in the diagram below are all in the pack before discarding the packing materials.

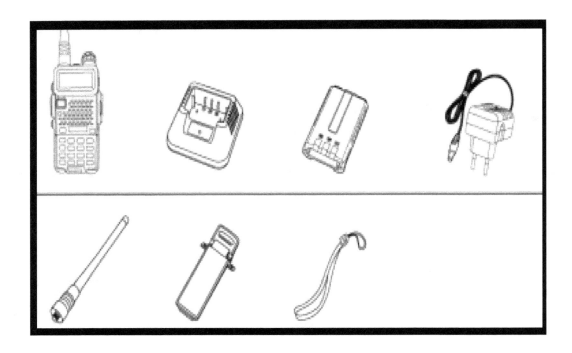

If any part is missing or damaged during the shipping, you can contact the dealer or your supplier promptly.

Optional Accessories to use with your Baofeng Radio:

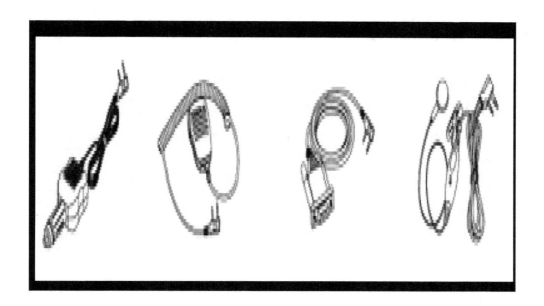

Installing The Accessories For Your Radio

Baofeng radios, such as the popular UV-5R model, are versatile devices that can be enhanced with a range of accessories. These accessories can expand the functionality of the radio, improve its performance, and tailor it to specific needs. Below is a detailed guide on how to install various accessories for Baofeng radios.

Antenna Installation

There are different types of Antennas:

- Standard Antenna: The default antenna that comes with the radio.
- HighGain Antenna: For extended range and better signal quality.
- Short Stubby Antenna: For compactness and portability.

To install Antenna, follow this steps:

1. Turn Off the Radio: Ensure the radio is turned off to prevent any damage during the installation.
2. Remove the Existing Antenna: Unscrew the existing antenna by rotating it counterclockwise.
3. Install the New Antenna: Screw the new antenna onto the radio by rotating it clockwise until it is snug. Do not over tighten, as this can damage the antenna or the radio's connector.

Battery Installation and Replacement

Various Types of Batteries:

- Standard Battery: Typically included with the radio.
- Extended Battery: Offers longer usage time between charges.

To install Battery On your radio follow this steps:

1. Remove the Old Battery:
   - Turn off the radio.
   - Press the battery release latch located at the bottom or back of the radio.
   - Slide the battery off the radio.

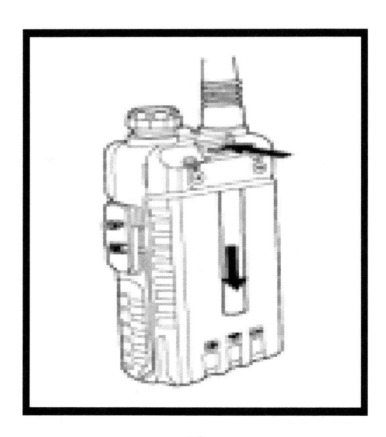

2. Install the New Battery:
- Align the new battery with the battery compartment.
- Slide the battery upward until it clicks into place.
- Ensure the battery is securely attached.

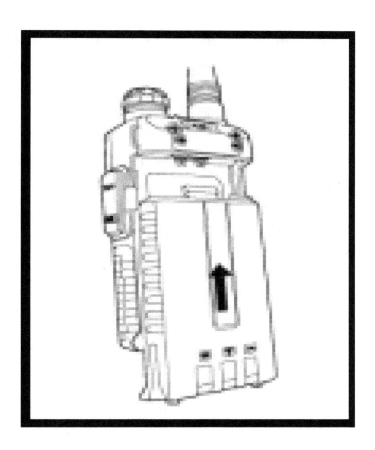

Installing Speaker/Microphone

Types of Speaker/Microphones includes:

- Standard Handheld Mic: For handheld use.
- Lapel Mic: Clips onto clothing for handsfree use.

To install Speakers/Microphone, follow these Steps:

1. Locate the Accessory Jack: The accessory jack is typically on the side of the radio, covered by a rubber flap.
2. Open the Accessory Jack Cover: Lift or rotate the rubber cover to expose the jack.
3. Insert the Connector: Plug the microphone or speaker connector into the jack. Ensure it is fully inserted for proper functionality.
4. Secure the Cable: Clip or secure the cable to your clothing to prevent it from snagging or pulling.

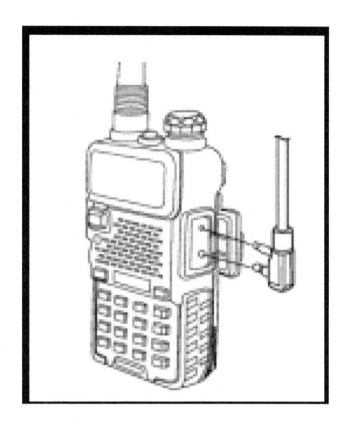

Installing Programming Cable

The Baofeng Radio comes with a USB Programming Cable that is used for connecting the radio to a computer for programming.

To Install The programming Cable:

1. Locate the Programming Jack: Similar to the speaker/microphone jack, this is often found on the side of the radio.

2. Open the Jack Cover: Lift or rotate the rubber cover to expose the jack.
3. Connect the Cable: Insert the programming cable into the jack. Ensure it is fully inserted.
4. Connect to Computer: Plug the USB end of the cable into your computer's USB port.
5. Install Drivers and Software: Follow the instructions provided with the cable to install any necessary drivers and programming software.

Headset Installation

Two types of Headsets to use with your radio:

- Standard Earpiece: For discreet listening.
- Over-the-Head Headset: For extended use and better audio quality.

Install Headset by following these steps:

1. Locate the Accessory Jack: Usually the same jack used for the speaker/microphone.
2. Open the Jack Cover: Lift or rotate the rubber cover to expose the jack.
3. Insert the Headset Connector: Plug the headset connector into the accessory jack.

4. Adjust the Headset: Position the earpiece or headset comfortably on your ear or head and adjust the microphone if needed.

Car Charger Installation

Install a "Standard Car Charger" that can be Plugged into a vehicle's cigarette lighter or power port.

1. Connect to Radio: Insert the charger connector into the radio's charging port.
2. Connect to Power Source: Plug the other end of the charger into the vehicle's cigarette lighter or power port.
3. Monitor Charging: Ensure the radio indicates charging (usually via an LED light).

Belt Clip Installation

There are different types of Belt Clips. Use a "Standard Belt Clip" that's typically included with the radio or replace with the same type if there's a damage or you have sneed for replacement.

1. Locate the Screw Holes: The screw holes for the belt clip are usually on the back of the radio.
2. Align the Belt Clip: Place the belt clip over the screw holes.

3. Secure the Clip: Use the screws provided to attach the belt clip to the radio. Tighten the screws until the belt clip is securely attached.

Hand Strap Installation

A "Standard Hand Strap" is recommended to provide a secure grip on the radio.

1. Attach to Loop: Thread the strap through the designated loop on the radio, usually found on the side or bottom.

2. Secure the Strap: Pull the strap through until it is tight and secure.

By following these detailed steps, you can effectively install and utilize various accessories to enhance the functionality and performance of your Baofeng radio. Whether it's extending the range with a high-gain antenna, ensuring continuous power with an extended battery, or facilitating hands-free communication with a headset, the right accessories can significantly improve your Baofeng radio experience.

Design and Specifications:

The design and specifications of Baofeng radios encompass various aspects of their physical construction, functionality, and technical characteristics. Understanding these elements is essential for users to fully appreciate the capabilities and performance of Baofeng handheld transceivers. Let's delve into this topic in detail, discussing what the design and specifications entail and providing a comprehensive list with explanations and examples:

Design of Baofeng Radios:

Ergonomic Design: Baofeng radios feature ergonomic designs with contoured grips and intuitive button layouts for comfortable handling and easy operation. The Baofeng UV-5R series is known for its compact size and user-friendly interface, making it popular among radio enthusiasts.

Durable Construction: Baofeng radios are built with robust materials and construction methods to withstand rugged conditions and outdoor use. Baofeng radios feature durable plastic or metal housings, reinforced antennas, and water-resistant seals for enhanced durability.

LCD Display: Baofeng radios are equipped with LCD displays that provide clear visibility of channel information, signal strength, battery status, and menu settings. The LCD display on Baofeng radios typically includes backlighting for visibility in low-light conditions and adjustable contrast settings.

Keypad and Controls: Baofeng radios have tactile keypads and controls for easy navigation and operation, including Push-To-Talk (PTT) buttons, function keys, and menu navigation buttons. The keypad layout on Baofeng radios is designed for intuitive access to essential functions such as channel selection, volume control, and menu navigation.

Antenna Design: Baofeng radios feature removable antennas with various lengths and configurations to optimize signal transmission and reception performance. Your Baofeng radios may come with a flexible rubber duck antenna for general use or an extended high-gain antenna for increased range.

Specifications of Baofeng Radios:

Frequency Range: Baofeng radios operate within specific frequency ranges, including VHF (Very High Frequency) and UHF (Ultra High Frequency) bands.

- The Baofeng UV-5R supports frequencies ranging from 136 to 174 MHz (VHF) and 400 to 520 MHz (UHF).

Channel Capacity: Baofeng radios can store and access multiple channels for communication, with varying capacities depending on the model.

- The Baofeng UV-82 can store up to 128 programmable channels for convenient access to frequently used frequencies.

Output Power: Baofeng radios emit radio signals at specific power levels, measured in watts (W), to transmit communication over varying distances.

- Baofeng radios typically offer adjustable output power levels, such as low (1 W) and high (5 W), to conserve battery or extend range as needed.

Modulation Type: Baofeng radios use specific modulation techniques, such as Frequency Modulation (FM), to encode voice or data signals for transmission.

- Baofeng radios utilize FM modulation to transmit and receive voice communications with high clarity and reliability.

Battery Capacity: Baofeng radios are powered by rechargeable lithium-ion batteries with specific capacities to provide operating time between charges.

- The Baofeng BF-F8HP comes with a 2000mAh battery for extended usage in demanding environments.

Dimensions and Weight: Baofeng radios have varying dimensions and weights, which affect their portability and suitability for different applications.

- The Baofeng UV-5R measures approximately 115 x 60 x 33 mm and weighs around 220 grams, making it compact and lightweight for handheld use.

Receiver Sensitivity: Baofeng radios feature receiver sensitivity specifications that determine their ability to detect weak signals and maintain communication under challenging conditions.

- Baofeng radios with high receiver sensitivity can pick up faint signals with minimal interference, ensuring reliable communication in noisy or congested environments.

Water Resistance Rating: Some Baofeng radios are designed with water resistance ratings, indicating their ability to withstand exposure to moisture or splashes.

- The Baofeng BF-F8HP is rated IP54, meaning it offers limited protection against dust ingress and water splashes.

Advanced Features for Technicians

Programming Flexibility: Baofeng radios offer extensive programming options, allowing technicians to fine-tune frequencies, set up repeaters, and customize channels for specific needs.

Firmware Updates: Stay on the cutting edge with insights into firmware updates. Learn how to keep your Baofeng radio up-to-date with the latest features and improvements.

This overview sets the stage for a deep dive into the world of Baofeng radios. Whether you're a technician seeking technical insights or an enthusiast eager to grasp the essence of these devices, the following chapters will unravel the layers of Baofeng's technological tapestry, empowering you to maximize the potential of your radio.

Components and Features Of Baofeng Radio

1. **Display Panel:** The display panel is the visual interface of your Baofeng radio, presenting critical information such as channel, frequency, signal strength, and battery status.

Look for the screen with alphanumeric characters, symbols, and possibly a backlight for visibility.

To set up:

- Navigate through the menu using designated buttons.
- Adjust contrast and backlight settings for optimal visibility.

2. **Buttons and Controls:** These include power, volume, channel selection, and function buttons. Each has a specific role in navigating and operating the radio. You can Locate buttons labeled for power, volume, channel up/down, and menu functions.

Setting Up:

- Power on/off: Press and hold the power button.
- Adjust volume: Rotate the volume knob.
- Navigate channels: Use channel up/down buttons.

3. **Antenna and Battery:** What they are: The antenna is essential for signal transmission, while the battery powers the radio. Identify the extendable antenna and the battery compartment.

Battery Charging

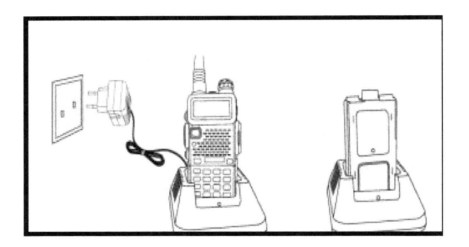

Setting Up:

Install the battery following the user manual guidelines.
- Extend the antenna fully for optimal performance.

Procedure for Setting Up:

1. **Display Panel:**
   - Power on the radio.
   - Navigate to the menu using dedicated buttons.
   - Adjust display settings, contrast, and backlight as preferred.

2. **Buttons and Controls:**

   - Familiarize yourself with the location of power, volume, and channel buttons.
   - Power on the radio and adjust the volume to a comfortable level.
   - Use channel up/down buttons to navigate to your desired frequency.

3. **Antenna and Battery:**

   - Install the battery following steps shown above.
   - Extend the antenna fully.
   - Monitor battery levels regularly and recharge or replace as necessary.

Mastering the radio components and features of your Baofeng device is foundational to efficient operation. Regular practice, customization, and a nuanced understanding of each element will empower you to make the most of your radio, whether for recreational use, professional applications, or emergency scenarios.

Deciphering the Components and Features of Your Baofeng Radio

Understanding the various components and features of your Baofeng radio is pivotal to harnessing its full potential. This section delves into each element with precision, offering clarity on identification, setup procedures, and effective usage.

1. Display Panel:

The display panel serves as the visual interface, presenting critical information such as the current channel, frequency, signal strength, battery status, and activated features or modes.

Locate the rectangular screen on the front face of your radio, typically adorned with alphanumeric characters, symbols, and possibly a backlight for enhanced visibility.

Setting Up:

- Power On/Off: Press and hold the power button to activate or deactivate the display and the radio.

- Contrast Adjustment: Navigate to the settings menu using the designated buttons, then select the display settings to adjust contrast.
- Backlight Control: Adjust backlight settings to optimize visibility in various lighting conditions.

2. Buttons and Controls:

The buttons and controls are the tactile interface of your radio, facilitating various functions such as power control, volume adjustment, channel selection, and menu navigation.

Baofeng Radio comes Identify the array of buttons labeled for power, volume, channel selection (up/down), and menu functions, located either on the front face or sides of the radio.

Setting Up:

- Power On/Off: Press and hold the power button to toggle the radio.
- Volume Adjustment: Rotate the volume knob to increase or decrease volume levels.
- Channel Selection: Use the channel up/down buttons to navigate through programmed channels or frequencies.
- Function Buttons: Familiarize yourself with buttons assigned to specific functions and features, such as scanning, dual watch, or emergency alerts.

3. Antenna and Battery:

The antenna and battery are fundamental components ensuring signal transmission and powering the radio, respectively.

- Keep the antenna extended during use to maximize signal strength. Monitor battery levels regularly and recharge or replace as necessary to ensure uninterrupted communication.

By meticulously understanding and mastering each component and feature of your Baofeng radio, you pave the way for efficient and effective communication. Regular practice, customization, and a nuanced approach to utilizing these elements will empower you to harness the full potential of your radio across various scenarios and environments.

Chapter Three

Understanding The Features of Baofeng Radio

The Baofeng radio is renowned for its versatility, combining advanced functionalities with user-friendly design. Below are the prominent features that set Baofeng radios apart in the world of two-way communication:

1. Frequency Range:
 - **VHF/UHF Support:** Most Baofeng radios offer dual-band support, covering both Very High Frequency (VHF) and Ultra High Frequency (UHF) bands, allowing for flexible communication across various channels and frequencies.

2. Power Output:
 - **Adjustable Power Levels:** Baofeng radios typically feature adjustable power output settings, allowing users to optimize transmission power based on the distance and communication requirements.

3. Channel Capacity:
 - **Multiple Channels:** With a vast channel capacity, Baofeng radios enable users to program and store numerous channels,

facilitating seamless switching between frequencies for different communication needs.

4. Display and Interface:

- **LCD Display:** Equipped with a clear LCD display, Baofeng radios provide real-time information on channel, frequency, battery status, and activated features, ensuring users are always informed.
- **User-Friendly Interface:** Intuitive button layout and menu navigation make Baofeng radios accessible and straightforward to operate, even for beginners.

5. Battery Life and Management:

- High-Capacity Battery Options: Baofeng radios come with varying battery capacities, with some models offering high-capacity options for extended use.
- Battery-Saving Features: Incorporating energy-efficient technologies, Baofeng radios optimize battery consumption to prolong operational duration.

6. Advanced Features:

- Scanning Modes: Baofeng radios offer scanning functionalities, allowing users to scan and monitor multiple channels for activity.
- VOX (Voice Operated Transmission): Enables hands-free operation by transmitting when the user speaks, enhancing convenience during communication.

- Dual Watch/Dual Reception: Allows users to monitor two channels simultaneously, ensuring no communication is missed.

7. Programming and Customization:
- Programmable Buttons: Baofeng radios feature programmable buttons, enabling users to customize and assign specific functions or features for quick access.
- PC Programming: With software support, users can program Baofeng radios via a computer, streamlining the channel setup and customization process.

8. Durability and Design:
- Robust Build: Constructed with durable materials, Baofeng radios are designed to withstand rugged use and challenging environments.
- Compact and Portable: Despite their feature-rich nature, Baofeng radios maintain a compact and portable design, ideal for outdoor adventures, professional use, and emergency situations.

9. Emergency Features:
- Emergency Alerts: Some Baofeng radio models come equipped with emergency alert features, allowing users to send distress signals or alarms when in need of assistance.
- Flashlight and Additional Tools: Incorporation of a built-in flashlight and other utility tools in certain models enhances the practicality and utility of Baofeng radios in various scenarios.

The comprehensive suite of features offered by Baofeng radios underscores their versatility and adaptability to diverse communication needs. Whether you are an outdoor enthusiast, a professional, or someone seeking reliable communication in emergencies, Baofeng radios stand as a dependable companion, ensuring seamless and effective communication across various channels and scenarios.

The Display Panel of Baofeng Radio

The display panel of a Baofeng radio serves as the user's primary interface, providing vital information about the radio's status, current settings, and operational parameters. Understanding the display panel is crucial for effective operation and maximizing the utility of your Baofeng radio.

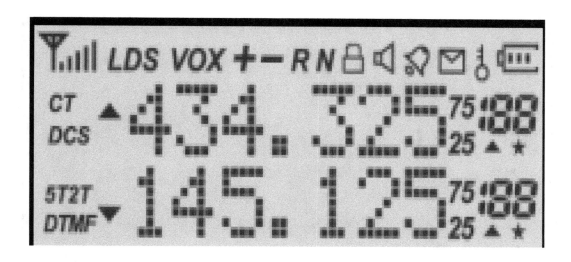

Display Panel Features:

LCD Screen: The Liquid Crystal Display (LCD) screen typically presents alphanumeric characters, channel numbers, frequency readings, and various symbols or icons to indicate operational modes, battery status, and signal strength.

Backlight: Many Baofeng radios come equipped with a backlight that illuminates the display, enhancing visibility in low-light conditions.

Indicator Icons: These are graphical representations that convey information about features such as battery status, signal reception, transmission mode, and activated functions or settings.

Accessing the Display Panel:

Accessing the display panel on a Baofeng radio is straightforward:

1. **Power On/Off:** Press and hold the power button to activate the radio and display panel. Repeat the process to power off.

2. **Mode Selection:** Use the mode or function button to toggle between different operational modes, such as frequency mode, channel mode, and menu mode, each of which displays relevant information on the LCD screen.

Setting Up the Display Panel:

Customizing the display panel to suit your preferences and operational needs can enhance user experience and efficiency. Here's how you can set up the display panel on a Baofeng radio:

1. **Contrast Adjustment:**
   - Access the menu by pressing the menu button.
   - Navigate to the display settings using the up/down arrow buttons.
   - Select the contrast adjustment option and use the arrow buttons to increase or decrease contrast levels.

2. **Backlight Control:**
   Access the menu and navigate to the display settings.
   Select the backlight option and adjust the backlight duration or intensity based on your preference.

3. **Channel/Frequency Display:**

Toggle between channel and frequency modes using the mode or function button to display either channel numbers or frequency readings on the LCD screen.

4. **Battery Status Indicator:**

Monitor the battery status indicator icon on the display panel to keep track of remaining battery life. Consider adjusting backlight settings to conserve battery power if needed.

Baofeng Radio Buttons and Controls

Understanding the buttons and controls of your Baofeng radio is essential for efficient operation and maximizing its functionalities. Below is a detailed overview of the commonly found buttons and controls on Baofeng radios, their functions, and how to access them.

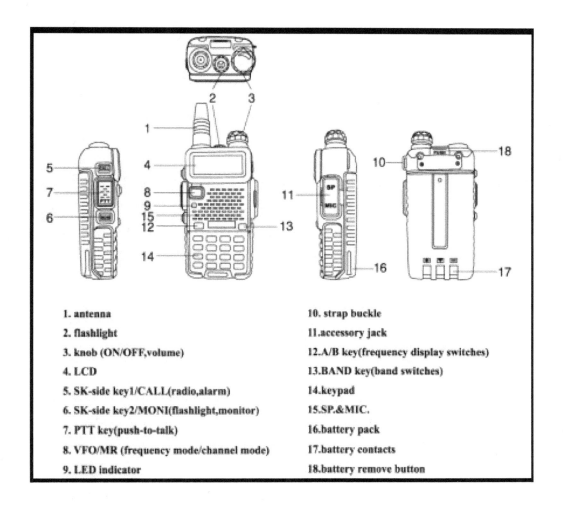

1. antenna	10. strap buckle
2. flashlight	11.accessory jack
3. knob (ON/OFF,volume)	12.A/B key(frequency display switches)
4. LCD	13.BAND key(band switches)
5. SK-side key1/CALL(radio,alarm)	14.keypad
6. SK-side key2/MONI(flashlight,monitor)	15.SP.&MIC.
7. PTT key(push-to-talk)	16.battery pack
8. VFO/MR (frequency mode/channel mode)	17.battery contacts
9. LED indicator	18.battery remove button

Power Button: The power button is used to turn the radio on and off.

- Access: Located usually at the top or side of the radio, pressing and holding this button for a few seconds will toggle the power state of the radio.

Volume Knob: The volume knob is used to adjust the audio output level of the radio.

- Access: Found typically on the top or side of the radio, rotating the knob clockwise increases the volume, while rotating it counterclockwise decreases the volume.

Channel/Menu Button: This multifunctional button toggles between different operational modes, such as channel mode, frequency mode, and menu mode, and also accesses the menu for setting adjustments.

- Access: Located usually on the front face of the radio, pressing this button cycles through the available modes or accesses the menu when held down.

Up/Down Arrow Buttons: These buttons are used for navigating through channels, frequencies, menu options, and adjusting settings.

- Access: Located typically on the front face of the radio, pressing the up arrow button scrolls up through channels, frequencies, or menu options, while the down arrow button scrolls down.

Function Buttons (F1, F2, F3, etc.):

These buttons are programmable and can be customized to perform specific functions or activate features such as scanning, dual watch, emergency alerts, and more.

- Access: Found usually on the front face or sides of the radio, pressing a function button activates the assigned function or feature.

Push-to-Talk (PTT) Button: The Push-to-Talk button is used to transmit your voice over the selected channel or frequency.

- Access: Located typically on the side of the radio, pressing and holding this button allows you to speak, and releasing it stops transmission.

Monitor Button: The Monitor button temporarily disables the squelch control to allow you to hear weak signals or background noise.

- Access: Found usually on the front face or sides of the radio, pressing this button momentarily deactivates the squelch.

8. **Lock Button:** The Lock button is used to lock the radio's buttons to prevent accidental changes to settings or channels.

- Access: Located typically on the side or front face of the radio, pressing and holding this button activates or deactivates the button lock feature.

Familiarizing yourself with the buttons and controls of your Baofeng radio, understanding their functions, and knowing how to access them efficiently is crucial for seamless operation and optimal utilization of your radio's capabilities. Regular practice and customization of programmable buttons can further enhance your user experience and enable you to tailor the radio's functionality to meet your specific communication needs across various scenarios and environments.

Antenna and Battery of Baofeng Radio

Understanding How the antenna and battery of your Baofeng radio works is essential for ensuring optimal performance and uninterrupted communication. Below is a detailed overview of these components, their functions, and how to access and set them up.

1. Antenna:

The antenna is responsible for transmitting and receiving radio signals, allowing for communication over various frequencies. The antenna is usually an integral part of the radio and cannot be removed permanently. However, some Baofeng radios may come with detachable antennas for customization or replacement. Simply extend the antenna fully to maximize signal reception and transmission performance. Ensure that the antenna is securely attached to the radio to prevent any signal loss or interference.

2. Battery:

The battery provides power to the Baofeng radio, enabling it to function wirelessly. The battery is typically housed in a compartment located on the back or bottom of the radio. It can be accessed by sliding or opening the battery cover.

To install or replace the battery:

- Slide or open the battery cover to access the battery compartment.
- Insert the battery into the compartment, ensuring that the polarity matches the markings inside.
- Close or slide the battery cover back into place until it clicks securely.

Battery Types:

1. Rechargeable Batteries: Baofeng radios often come with rechargeable lithium-ion batteries, which can be charged using a compatible charger.

2. AA Batteries: Some Baofeng models may also support AA batteries, providing a convenient alternative power source when rechargeable batteries are unavailable.

Battery Management:

Charging: To charge the battery, remove it from the radio and insert it into the charger provided with the radio. Follow the manufacturer's instructions for charging times and precautions.

Battery Life: Monitor the battery life indicator on the display panel to gauge remaining battery capacity. Recharge or replace the battery as needed to ensure uninterrupted communication.

Additional Tips:

- Battery Conservation: To conserve battery life, adjust the radio's power output settings and use energy-saving features such as low-power mode when appropriate.

- Battery Safety: Follow proper battery handling and storage practices to prevent damage or accidents. Avoid exposing the battery to extreme temperatures or moisture.

The antenna and battery are integral components of your Baofeng radio, ensuring reliable communication and power supply. By understanding how to access and set up these components correctly, as well as implementing proper battery management practices, you can optimize the performance and longevity of your Baofeng radio, ensuring seamless communication in various scenarios and environments.

Chapter Four:

Initial Setup and Configuration of Your Baofeng Radio

In this pivotal chapter, we embark on the foundational journey of setting up and configuring your Baofeng radio. As we delve into the intricacies of initialization, channel programming, and essential settings, you'll lay the groundwork for seamless communication across various frequencies and channels. Whether you're unboxing your Baofeng radio for the first time or seeking to fine-tune its settings for optimal performance, this chapter serves as your guiding beacon. Let's embark on this voyage of discovery and mastery as we navigate the initial setup and configuration of your Baofeng radio.

1. **Battery Installation/Setup**:

Installing the battery is the first step in setting up your Baofeng radio, ensuring it has the power to function.

- Slide or open the battery compartment cover located on the back or bottom of the radio.

- Insert the battery into the compartment, ensuring the correct polarity.
- Close or slide the battery cover back into place securely.

Programming Channels:

Programming channels allows you to store frequently used frequencies for quick and easy access.

- Press the menu button to access the menu.
- Navigate to the channel programming option using the up/down arrow buttons.
- Select the desired channel number or position.
- Enter the frequency using the numeric keypad.
- Save the programmed frequency to the selected channel number.

Setting the Squelch:

Adjusting the squelch threshold helps reduce background noise and interference, ensuring clear communication.

- Access the menu and navigate to the squelch settings.
- Adjust the squelch level using the up/down arrow buttons.

- Monitor the signal indicator on the display panel to gauge the effectiveness of the squelch setting.
- Fine-tune the squelch level until background noise is minimized without affecting signal reception.

Setting Transmit Power

Adjusting the transmit power level allows you to optimize battery life and signal strength based on your communication needs.

- Access the menu and navigate to the transmit power settings.
- Select the desired power level (low, medium, or high) based on the communication range and battery conservation requirements.

Scanning and Monitoring:

Scanning and monitoring functionalities allow you to search for active channels and monitor multiple frequencies simultaneously.

- Press the scan button to initiate the scanning process.
- Monitor the display panel for active channels or frequencies.

- Press the monitor button to temporarily disable the squelch and listen for weak signals or background noise.

Customizing Settings:

Customizing settings enables you to tailor the radio's functionality to your specific preferences and operational requirements.

- Access the menu and navigate to the settings you wish to customize.
- Use the up/down arrow buttons to adjust the settings according to your preferences.
- Save the customized settings to ensure they are retained for future use.

Mastering the initial setup and configuration of your Baofeng radio is essential for unlocking its full potential and ensuring seamless communication. By following the detailed procedures outlined above, you'll be equipped to customize your radio to meet your specific needs and navigate various communication scenarios with confidence and ease.

Basic Operations of Your Baofeng Radio

Understanding the basic functions of your Baofeng radio is essential for effortless and effective communication. Below, we explore the core functions of your radio, detailing their definitions, operational mechanics, and access methods.

1. **Power On/Off:** The power function controls the radio's operational state, either activating or deactivating its functionalities.

To power on/off the radio, press and hold the designated power button until the display illuminates or turns off, indicating the radio's status.

The power button is typically located on the top, side, or front panel of the radio, easily accessible for immediate use.

2. **Volume Control**: Volume control governs the audio output level of the radio, enabling comfortable listening based on environmental conditions and personal preferences.

Rotate the volume knob clockwise to increase and counterclockwise to decrease the audio volume.

The volume knob is prominently positioned on the radio's front or side panel, facilitating quick and intuitive adjustments.

3. **Channel Selection:** Channel selection permits users to switch between different pre-programmed channels or frequencies for communication.

- Navigate through the available channels using the up/down arrow buttons or directly input the channel number using the numeric keypad.

Channel selection is accessed via dedicated buttons or through the radio's menu interface, providing easy access to stored channels.

4. **Transmit and Receive**: The transmit/receive function facilitates voice or data communication by enabling transmission and reception capabilities over the selected channel or frequency.

- Press and hold the Push-to-Talk (PTT) button to transmit messages; release the button to switch to receiving mode and listen to incoming communications.

- The PTT button is typically located on the side or front panel of the radio, easily accessible for initiating transmissions.

5. **Squelch Control:** Squelch control minimizes background noise and interference, optimizing the clarity and quality of received signals.

- Adjust the squelch level via the menu settings or dedicated squelch button to filter out unwanted noise without compromising signal reception.

- Squelch control can be accessed through the radio's menu interface or via a dedicated squelch button, providing tailored noise reduction based on user preferences.

6. Scanning and Monitoring: Scanning and monitoring functionalities enable users to search for active channels, frequencies, or signals and monitor multiple channels simultaneously.

- **Operation**: Initiate the scanning process by pressing the scan button or activate monitoring mode to listen for weak signals or background noise.

- **Access Method**: Scanning and monitoring features can be accessed through dedicated buttons or menu options, allowing users to customize scanning parameters and monitor specific channels or frequencies.

Familiarizing yourself with the basic functions of your Baofeng radio is fundamental for maximizing its utility and ensuring seamless communication across various scenarios. By understanding the definitions, operational mechanics, and access methods of each function, you can confidently navigate your radio's capabilities, customize settings to meet specific needs, and leverage its full potential for reliable and effective communication.

Understanding CTSS and DCS Codes in Baofeng Radio

CTSS (Continuous Tone-Coded Squelch System) and DCS (Digital-Coded Squelch) codes are sub-audible tone signals used to prevent receiving unwanted transmissions on the same frequency. These codes help filter out interference and allow only radios programmed with the same CTSS or DCS code to communicate with each other.

What are CTSS and DCS Codes?

- CTSS (Continuous Tone-Coded Squelch System):
- CTSS codes use a continuous tone at a specific frequency to open the squelch on a receiving radio, allowing communication only from radios transmitting the same tone.

DCS (Digital-Coded Squelch): DCS codes use a series of digital tones to encode information, enabling more secure and versatile squelch control compared to CTSS.

How to Identify CTSS and DCS Codes

CTSS: CTSS codes are typically represented by a frequency value (e.g., 67.0 Hz, 123.0 Hz) corresponding to the specific tone used for squelch control.

DCS: DCS codes are represented by a combination of three-digit numbers or alphanumeric codes, each corresponding to a specific digital tone sequence.

How to Access CTSS and DCS Codes

To access CTSS AND DCS codes, navigate to the radio's menu settings related to squelch control or tone settings to access CTSS and DCS code options.

Examples:

- To access CTSS codes: Menu > Squelch/Tone Settings > CTSS > Select desired frequency (e.g., 67.0 Hz).
- To access DCS codes: Menu > Squelch/Tone Settings > DCS > Select desired code (e.g., DCS 023).

Setup and Configuration of CTSS and DCS Codes

To Configure and Setup CTSS and DCS Codes:

Select the desired CTSS or DCS code based on your communication requirements and ensure that all radios within your group are programmed with the same code for seamless communication, and then enable CTSS or DCS squelch control in the menu settings and input the selected code to activate the feature.

Examples:

You can do your CTSS Configuration by following these steps:
- Go to Menu > Squelch/Tone Settings > CTSS > Enable > Select frequency (e.g., 67.0 Hz) > Save.

For DCS Configuration:
- Menu > Squelch/Tone Settings > DCS > Enable > Select code (e.g., DCS 023) > Save.

Understanding and implementing CTSS and DCS codes in your Baofeng radio can significantly enhance your communication experience by reducing interference and ensuring secure and clear transmissions. By familiarizing yourself with these codes, identifying their representation, accessing them through menu `settings, and configuring them correctly, you can optimize your radio's squelch control and enjoy reliable and interference-free communication with your group or network.

Understanding Dual Watch and Dual Reception in Baofeng Radio

Dual Watch and Dual Reception are advanced features available in Baofeng radios, allowing users to monitor multiple channels simultaneously for increased situational awareness and flexibility in communication.

What are Dual Watch and Dual Reception?

Dual Watch: Dual Watch is a feature that enables the radio to monitor two channels alternately, switching between them at predetermined intervals or when activity is detected on either channel.

Dual Reception: The Dual Reception feature allows the radio to receive signals on two channels simultaneously, enabling users to monitor both channels concurrently without missing any transmissions.

How to Identify Dual Watch and Dual Reception

The Dual Watch mode is typically indicated by a DW icon or indicator on the radio's display panel when activated, and Dual Reception mode may also be indicated by a DR icon or indicator on the display panel when activated.

How to Access Dual Watch and Dual Reception

To access Dual Watch and Dual Reception:

Navigate to the radio's menu settings related to channel monitoring or reception modes to access Dual Watch and Dual Reception options.

Setup and Configuration of Dual Watch and Dual Reception:

To Setup Dual Watch and Dual Reception:
- Determine the desired channels to monitor or receive simultaneously and ensure they are programmed and stored in the radio.

- Enable Dual Watch or Dual Reception mode in the menu settings and select the channels to monitor or receive concurrently.

For example:

For Dual Watch Setup:

Menu > Channel/Mode Settings > Dual Watch > Enable > Select primary and secondary channels > Set watch interval (if applicable) > Save.

Dual Reception Setup:

Menu > Channel/Mode Settings > Dual Reception > Enable > Select primary and secondary channels > Save.

Dual Watch and Dual Reception features provide enhanced monitoring capabilities and flexibility in communication, allowing Baofeng radio users to stay informed and responsive in dynamic environments. By understanding these features, identifying their activation indicators, accessing them through menu settings, and configuring them according to specific needs, users can maximize their radio's functionality and adaptability for various communication scenarios with ease and efficiency.

Chapter Five
Programming Baofeng Radio

Programming a Baofeng radio involves setting up and configuring various parameters such as frequencies, channels, CTSS/DCS codes, and other settings to suit specific communication requirements. Proper programming ensures seamless and effective communication, allowing users to utilize their Baofeng radios to their full potential.

Programming refers to the process of customizing and configuring a Baofeng radio's settings, channels, frequencies, and other features to meet specific communication needs and operational requirements.

Ways to Program Your Baofeng Radio:

Manual Programming:
Manual programming involves directly inputting frequencies, channels, and other settings using the radio's keypad and menu interface.

Software Programming:

Software programming utilizes computer software and a programming cable to program the radio via a computer, offering a more efficient and organized method for programming multiple channels and settings.

Programming The Software:

- CHIRP (Comprehensive Ham Radio Programming Software)
- Baofeng official software (OEM software provided by Baofeng)
- Other third-party software compatible with Baofeng radios.

3. Examples of Manual Programming:

o Programming a Frequency:

- Turn on the radio and navigate to the menu.
- Select the frequency mode and enter the desired frequency using the keypad.
- Save the programmed frequency to a vacant channel number.

o Setting CTSS/DCS Codes:

- Access the menu and navigate to the tone or squelch settings.
- Select CTSS or DCS and input the desired code or frequency.
- Save the programmed code to the respective channel or frequency.

4. Examples of Software Programming:

o Using CHIRP:

Install and open CHIRP software on your computer.

- Connect the Baofeng radio to the computer using a programming cable.
- Download existing radio configuration or create a new one.
- Input frequencies, channels, CTSS/DCS codes, and other settings.
- Upload the programmed configuration to the radio.

Using Baofeng Official Software

Install the official Baofeng programming software on your computer.
- Connect the radio to the computer via a programming cable.
- Select the desired settings, frequencies, and channels.
- Upload the programmed configuration to the radio.

Programming a Baofeng radio is a fundamental process that empowers users to customize their radios according to specific communication needs and operational scenarios. Whether through manual programming using the radio's keypad and menu interface or software programming via computer software, mastering the programming process enables users to optimize their Baofeng radios' functionality, flexibility, and performance for reliable and effective communication across various environments and applications.

Software Programming of Baofeng Radio via Computer

Software programming of Baofeng radios via computer provides a streamlined and efficient method for configuring various settings, frequencies, and channels. This approach offers greater flexibility and organization compared to manual programming, allowing users to manage multiple radio configurations with ease. Let's delve into the process of software programming in detail.

Software programming involves using computer software to customize and configure a Baofeng radio's settings, frequencies, channels, and other features.

Various Ways to Perform Software Programming Includes:

- o **CHIRP (Comprehensive Ham Radio Programming Software):**

CHIRP is a popular and widely used software tool designed for programming various brands of ham radios, including Baofeng. It offers a user-friendly interface and supports a wide range of features, making it a preferred choice for many Baofeng radio users.

- ○ **Baofeng Official Software:**

Baofeng provides its own official programming software, specifically tailored for its line of radios. While not as feature-rich as CHIRP, the official software offers basic programming functionalities and is suitable for users who prefer an official solution.

Steps for Software Programming using CHIRP:

1. **Installation**:
   - Download and install CHIRP software on your computer from the official website.

2. **Connection**:
   - Use a programming cable to connect your Baofeng radio to the computer's USB port.

3. **Configuration Setup**:
   - Launch CHIRP software and select the Baofeng radio model from the list of supported devices.

- Choose whether to download the existing configuration from the radio or create a new one.

4. **Programming**:
- Input frequencies, channels, CTSS/DCS codes, and other settings using CHIRP's intuitive interface.
- Organize and arrange channels and settings according to your preferences.

5. **Upload to Radio**:
- Once programming is complete, upload the configured settings to the Baofeng radio using CHIRP.
- Disconnect the programming cable from the radio and computer once the upload is successful.

Steps for Software Programming using Baofeng Official Software:

1. **Installation**:
- Download and install the official Baofeng programming software on your computer from the Baofeng website or the accompanying CD.

2. **Connection**:
- Connect your Baofeng radio to the computer using a programming cable.

3. **Configuration Setup**:

- Launch the Baofeng official software and select the appropriate radio model from the menu.

4. **Programming**:
   - Input frequencies, channels, CTSS/DCS codes, and other settings using the software's interface.
   - Customize and organize the programming layout as desired.

   4. **Upload to Radio**:

   - Once programming is complete, upload the configured settings to the Baofeng radio using the official software.
   - Disconnect the programming cable from the radio and computer upon successful upload.

Software programming of Baofeng radios via computer offers a convenient and efficient method for configuring radio settings and channels. Whether using CHIRP or the official Baofeng software, mastering the software programming process empowers users to optimize their radios' functionality and tailor them to specific communication needs with ease and precision.

Storing and Naming Channels in Baofeng Radio

Storing and naming channels in a Baofeng radio involves saving specific frequencies, settings, and configurations for easy access and reference. Channels act as predefined placeholders for storing and organizing different frequencies, enabling users to quickly switch between various communication options. Naming channels further enhances organization by assigning descriptive labels to each stored frequency or configuration, facilitating intuitive navigation and usage.

Channels

Channels are predefined placeholders within a Baofeng radio's memory where specific frequencies, settings, and configurations are stored for quick and easy access.

How to Store and Name Channels in Baofeng Radio:

1. Manual Programming:

Directly input and save frequencies, CTSS/DCS codes, and other settings using the radio's keypad and menu interface.

2. **Software Programming:**
Utilize computer software such as CHIRP or Baofeng official software to organize, store, and name channels via a computer interface.

Use the Following Steps for Manual Storing and Naming of Channels:

1. Accessing Memory Mode:

Turn on the radio and navigate to the memory mode or channel storage section using the menu

Chapter Six

Exploring Advanced Features of Baofeng Radio

In this chapter, we explore the advanced features of Baofeng radios, unlocking their full potential for enhanced communication and functionality. From advanced settings to specialized functionalities, these features offer users greater flexibility and customization options. Let's delve into each advanced feature in detail, understanding its purpose, access methods, and practical applications.

The Advanced Features includes:

1. Dual Watch and Dual Reception
2. CTSS and DCS Squelch
3. Frequency Offset and Shift
4. VOX (Voice-Operated Transmission)
5. Priority Scan
6. FM Radio Reception
7. Emergency Alarm
8. Battery Saver Mode
9. Channel Scanning
10. Backlit Display

1. **Dual Watch and Dual Reception**: Dual Watch enables monitoring of two channels alternately, while Dual Reception allows simultaneous reception on two channels.

Access these features through the radio's menu settings or dedicated buttons.

- Dual Watch allows monitoring of a primary channel while periodically checking a secondary channel for activity.

2. **CTSS and DCS Squelch:** CTSS and DCS squelch systems filter out unwanted noise and interference by utilizing sub-audible tones or digital codes.

Configure CTSS/DCS codes through the radio's menu settings.

- Assigning a specific CTSS code to a channel ensures that only radios transmitting the same code can be heard on that channel.

3. **Frequency Offset and Shift:** Frequency offset allows users to transmit and receive on different frequencies while maintaining a consistent offset.

- Set frequency offset values in the radio's menu settings.

- Setting a frequency offset allows for operation on a repeater system, where they transmit and receive frequencies differ.

4. **VOX (Voice-Operated Transmission):** VOX automatically activates transmission when the radio detects voice input, eliminating the need for manual PTT operation.

- Enable VOX mode and adjust sensitivity levels in the radio's menu settings.

- VOX is useful in hands-free communication scenarios, such as operating a radio while performing other tasks.

5. **Priority Scan:** Priority Scan automatically checks a designated channel for activity while scanning other channels.

- Activate Priority Scan mode through the radio's menu settings or dedicated buttons.

- Assigning an emergency channel as priority ensures critical communications are not missed during scanning.

6. **FM Radio Reception:** Baofeng radios equipped with FM radio reception feature allow users to listen to FM radio broadcasts.

- Switch to FM radio mode through the radio's mode selection options.

- Listening to weather updates or music broadcasts on the FM radio during downtime.

7. **Emergency Alarm:** Activating the emergency alarm triggers a loud alert signal, notifying others of an emergency situation.

- Press the emergency alarm button or activate it through the radio's menu settings.

- Using the emergency alarm to signal distress or summon assistance in hazardous situations.

8. **Battery Saver Mode:** Battery Saver Mode conserves battery power by reducing radio activity during periods of inactivity.

- Enable Battery Saver Mode through the radio's menu settings.

- Extending battery life during prolonged use in remote locations or emergency situations.

9. **Channel Scanning:** Channel Scanning automatically scans through stored channels, searching for active transmissions.

- Initiate Channel Scan mode through the radio's menu settings or dedicated buttons.

- Quickly identifying active channels or frequencies without manual tuning.

10. **Backlit Display:** Backlit Display illuminates the radio's display panel for improved visibility in low-light conditions.

- Enable or adjust the backlight settings through the radio's menu settings.

- Enhancing visibility and readability of the display panel during nighttime operations or in dark environments.

Mastering the advanced features of Baofeng radios enhances communication capabilities and operational efficiency, enabling users to adapt to diverse scenarios and requirements. By understanding the purpose, access methods, and practical applications of each feature, users can leverage their Baofeng radios to their full potential, ensuring seamless and reliable communication in various environments and situations.

Repeater

A repeater is a radio communication device that receives signals on one frequency and retransmits them on another frequency, effectively extending the range of communication between users.

Repeater Usage in Baofeng Radio

Utilizing repeaters in Baofeng radios expands communication range and enhances signal coverage, particularly in areas with geographical obstacles or long distances between users.

Understanding repeater functionality, accessing repeater frequencies, and effectively utilizing them are essential for maximizing communication capabilities.

Types of Repeaters:

1. Analog Repeaters
2. Digital Repeaters

1. **Analog Repeaters:** Analog repeaters receive and retransmit analog signals, commonly used in traditional analog communication systems.

- Access analog repeaters by tuning into their specific frequencies, which are typically provided by repeater directories or clubs.

2. **Digital Repeaters:** Digital repeaters receive and retransmit digital signals, offering enhanced clarity and efficiency compared to analog repeaters.

- Access digital repeaters by tuning into their specific frequencies, which are also available through repeater directories or clubs.

How to Access and Use Repeaters:

1. **Manual Frequency Input:** Manually input the repeater's frequency into the Baofeng radio's keypad and configure necessary settings.

- Enter the repeater's frequency (input and output), offset, and tone codes directly into the radio's memory.

2. **Repeater Directory Lookup:** Refer to online repeater directories or databases to find repeater frequencies, locations, and other relevant information.

- Use websites or mobile apps dedicated to amateur radio repeaters to search for repeaters in your area or desired communication range.

3. **Software Programming:** Utilize radio programming software such as CHIRP to program repeater frequencies and settings into the Baofeng radio via computer interface.

- Create a channel list containing repeater frequencies and configurations, then upload the programming data to the radio using CHIRP software.

4. **Memory Channel Storage**: Store repeater frequencies and configurations as memory channels in the Baofeng radio's memory for quick and easy access.

- Save frequently used repeater frequencies with their associated settings (offset, tone codes) as dedicated memory channels in the radio's memory bank.

Practical Applications of Repeaters:

1. **Extending Communication Range:** Utilize repeaters to extend communication range and overcome obstacles such as terrain or buildings.

2. **Enhancing Signal Coverage:** Access repeaters strategically located in elevated positions to enhance signal coverage in urban or remote areas.

3. **Joining Amateur Radio Nets:** Participate in amateur radio nets by accessing repeaters used for organized group communications and events.

4. **Emergency Communications:** Use repeaters for emergency communications during natural disasters or other crisis situations where traditional communication methods may be unreliable.

By utilizing repeaters effectively through manual frequency input, repeater directory lookup, software programming, and memory channel storage, you can extend communication range, enhance signal coverage, and participate in various amateur radio activities with confidence and efficiency.

Emergency Features and SOS Signals in Baofeng Radio

Emergency features and SOS signals in Baofeng radios are critical functionalities designed to ensure user safety and facilitate timely assistance in emergency situations. These features enable users to quickly signal for help and enhance communication capabilities during crises. Let's explore the comprehensive list of emergency features and SOS signals, along with their descriptions, access methods, and practical applications.

Emergency Features and SOS Signals Includes:

1. Emergency Alarm
2. SOS Signal Transmission
3. Channel Monitoring
4. Priority Scan
5. Emergency Channel Programming
6. VOX (Voice-Operated Transmission) with Emergency Activation

1. Emergency Alarm:

The emergency alarm emits a loud alert signal to attract attention and notify others of an emergency situation.

Press the dedicated emergency alarm button on the Baofeng radio or activate it through the menu settings.

- Signaling distress or summoning assistance in hazardous situations such as accidents, medical emergencies, or outdoor emergencies.

2. SOS Signal Transmission:

The SOS signal is a standardized distress signal consisting of three short, three long, and three short audible tones

- Manually transmit the SOS signal using Morse code via the radio's PTT button or through dedicated SOS signal transmission settings.

- Signaling for urgent assistance or rescue in emergency situations where verbal communication may be limited or ineffective.

3. Channel Monitoring:

Channel monitoring enables users to listen for incoming transmissions on specific channels or frequencies.

- Activate channel monitoring mode through the radio's menu settings or dedicated buttons.

- Monitoring emergency channels or frequencies for incoming distress calls or assistance requests during crises.

4. Priority Scan:

Priority scan automatically checks a designated channel for activity while scanning other channels.

Enable priority scan mode through the radio's menu settings or dedicated buttons, assigning an emergency channel as priority.

- Ensuring critical communications are not missed by assigning an emergency channel as priority during scanning.

5. Emergency Channel Programming:

Dedicated programming of emergency channels or frequencies for quick access during emergencies.

- Program emergency channels manually or through software programming, storing them as memory channels in the radio's memory bank.

- **Practical Application:** Preparing for emergencies by programming dedicated channels for emergency communication and coordination.

6. VOX (Voice-Operated Transmission) with Emergency Activation:

VOX automatically activates transmission when the radio detects voice input, with an emergency activation feature for hands-free emergency communication.

- Enable VOX mode and emergency activation through the radio's menu settings, adjusting sensitivity levels as needed.

Practical Application: Facilitating hands-free communication in emergency situations, allowing users to transmit distress messages without manual PTT operation.

Emergency features and SOS signals in Baofeng radios are essential tools for ensuring user safety and effective communication during emergencies. By understanding the functionality, access methods, and practical applications of each feature, users can confidently utilize their Baofeng radios to signal for help, monitor emergency channels, and coordinate rescue efforts in critical situations, ultimately enhancing overall preparedness and response capabilities.

Chapter Seven

Troubleshooting in Baofeng Radio

Troubleshooting in Baofeng radios involves identifying and resolving common issues that users may encounter during operation. By understanding these issues and their potential causes, users can effectively troubleshoot and address them to ensure optimal performance and functionality of their radios.

Common Issues:

1. No Power
2. No Transmit or Receive
3. Poor Audio Quality
4. Interference or Static
5. Programming Errors
6. Battery Drain
7. Keypad Malfunction
8. Antenna Connection Issues
9. Frequency Drift
10.   Display or Backlight Issues

No Power: The radio does not power on when the power button is pressed.

- Check the battery or power source for proper connection and charge.
- Replace or recharge the battery if low or depleted.
- Ensure the power switch is in the "on" position.

No Transmit or Receive: The radio cannot transmit or receive signals.

- Check the antenna connection for secure attachment.
- Verify that the radio is tuned to the correct frequency and channel.
- Ensure that the squelch level is adjusted appropriately to allow reception.

Poor Audio Quality: Audio output is distorted, unclear, or muffled.

- Adjust the volume level to a suitable level.
- Check for obstructions or debris blocking the speaker or microphone.
- Verify that the microphone is positioned correctly and not obstructed.

Interference or Static: The radio receives interference or static noise.

- Change the channel or frequency to avoid interference.
- Adjust the squelch level to filter out unwanted noise.

- Ensure that nearby electronic devices are not causing interference.

Programming Errors: Programming errors result in incorrect channel settings or frequencies.

- Double-check the programmed frequencies and settings for accuracy.
- Use radio programming software to correct errors and reprogram the radio if necessary.
- Refer to the user manual or online resources for proper programming procedures.

Battery Drain: The radio's battery drains quickly or does not hold a charge.

- Replace the battery with a new or fully charged one.
- Check for battery-intensive features or settings that may be contributing to excessive drain.
- Ensure that the battery contacts are clean and making proper contact with the radio.

Keypad Malfunction: The radio's keypad buttons do not respond or function properly.

- Clean the keypad and surrounding area to remove dirt or debris.
- Ensure that the keypad lock feature is not activated.

- If the issue persists, contact customer support for further assistance or repair.

Antenna Connection Issues:

Poor antenna connection leads to weak or intermittent signal reception.

- Check the antenna connector for looseness or damage.
- Tighten the antenna connector securely to the radio.
- Consider using a different antenna to determine if the issue lies with the antenna itself.

Frequency Drift: The radio's frequency drifts or shifts unexpectedly.

- Perform a reset or calibration procedure as outlined in the user manual.
- Ensure that the radio is operated within its specified temperature range.
- Contact customer support if frequency drift persists despite troubleshooting efforts.

Display or Backlight Issues:

The radio's display screen or backlight does not function properly.

- Adjust the display contrast or brightness settings if applicable.
- Check for loose connections or damage to the display panel.
- Reset the radio to factory defaults to rule out software-related issues.

Troubleshooting in Baofeng radios involves identifying and resolving common issues that may arise during operation. By understanding the nature of these issues and following the appropriate troubleshooting steps, users can effectively address problems and maintain optimal performance and functionality of their radios. If issues persist despite troubleshooting efforts, contacting customer support or seeking professional assistance may be necessary to resolve more complex or hardware-related issues.

Firmware Updates

Firmware updates in Baofeng radios are essential for ensuring optimal performance, fixing bugs, and introducing new features. Understanding firmware updates, identifying when they are needed, and performing the update process correctly are crucial for maintaining the functionality and reliability of Baofeng radios.

Common Firmware Updates in Baofeng Radio includes:

1. Bug Fixes
2. Performance Enhancements
3. New Features Addition
4. Security Patches

1. Bug Fixes: Bug fixes address software issues or glitches that may affect the radio's performance or functionality.
- A firmware update may fix a bug that causes intermittent audio dropout during transmission.

2. Performance Enhancements: Performance enhancements optimize the radio's operation and improve efficiency.

- A firmware update may improve receiver sensitivity, resulting in better signal reception in weak signal areas.

3. New Features Addition: New features addition introduces additional functionalities or capabilities to the radio.

- A firmware update may add a squelch tail elimination feature, reducing noise after transmission.

4. Security Patches: Security patches address vulnerabilities or security issues in the radio's firmware.

- A firmware update may patch a vulnerability that could potentially be exploited by malicious parties to gain unauthorized access to the radio.

How to Deal with Firmware Updates on Baofeng Radio

1. **Check for Updates:** Regularly check Baofeng's official website or firmware update announcements for the latest firmware releases.
Visit Baofeng's website to see if any firmware updates are available for your radio model.

2. Download Firmware: Download the latest firmware version from a trusted source, such as Baofeng's official website. Download the firmware update file to your computer or mobile device.

3. Backup Settings: Before performing the firmware update, backup your radio's settings and configurations to avoid data loss. Use radio programming software like CHIRP to save your current settings to a computer file.

4. Update Firmware: Follow the instructions provided with the firmware update file to install the update onto your Baofeng radio.
   - Connect your radio to a computer using a programming cable and use software like CHIRP to upload the firmware update file to the radio.

5. **Verify Update:** After the firmware update is complete, verify that the update was successful and that the radio is functioning properly.

- Test various functions and features of the radio to ensure they are working correctly.

Examples of Firmware Updates:

1.**Bug Fix Update:** A firmware update resolves an issue where the radio intermittently freezes during operation.

2. **Performance Enhancement Update:** A firmware update improves the radio's battery life by optimizing power management algorithms.

3. **New Features Addition Update:** A firmware update adds a VOX (Voice-Activated Transmission) feature to the radio, allowing for hands-free operation.

4. **Security Patch Update:** A firmware update patches a security vulnerability that could potentially be exploited to remotely access the radio's settings.

Firmware updates are essential for maintaining the functionality, security, and performance of Baofeng radios. By understanding the different types of firmware updates, knowing how to check for updates, and following the correct procedures for performing updates, users can ensure that their radios are up-to-date and operating at their best. Regularly checking for firmware updates and staying informed about the latest releases is key to maximizing the potential of Baofeng radios and staying ahead of any potential issues or vulnerabilities.

Battery Management and Charging for Baofeng Radio

Effective battery management and charging are crucial for maintaining the performance and longevity of Baofeng radios. By following proper battery management practices, users can maximize the lifespan of their batteries, ensure reliable operation, and avoid downtime due to battery-related issues.

Battery Management Tips:

1. **Use Genuine Batteries:**
   - Use genuine Baofeng batteries or compatible batteries recommended by the manufacturer to ensure compatibility and optimal performance.
   - Avoid using counterfeit or low-quality batteries, as they may not provide reliable power or could damage the radio.

2. **Proper Charging:**

- Use the provided charger or a compatible charger designed for Baofeng radios to ensure proper charging.
- Follow manufacturer recommendations for charging times and procedures to prevent overcharging or undercharging the battery.

3. **Avoid Overcharging:**
   - Avoid leaving the battery connected to the charger for extended periods after it has reached full charge, as overcharging can degrade battery performance and shorten its lifespan.
   - Remove the battery from the charger once it is fully charged to prevent overcharging.

4. **Avoid Deep Discharging:**
   - Avoid fully discharging the battery whenever possible, as deep discharges can reduce battery capacity and lifespan.
   - Recharge the battery before it becomes completely depleted to prolong its lifespan and maintain optimal performance.

5. **Store Batteries Properly:**
   - Store batteries in a cool, dry place away from direct sunlight and extreme temperatures.
   - Avoid storing batteries in a discharged state for extended periods, as this can lead to capacity loss and performance degradation.

Charging Methods

1. **Direct Charging:**
   - Connect the Baofeng radio to the charger using the provided charging cable and plug it into a power source.
   - Follow manufacturer instructions for proper charging times and procedures.

2. **Desktop Charger:**
   - Use a desktop charger with multiple charging slots to charge multiple batteries simultaneously.
   - Place the battery in the charger slot and ensure proper alignment for charging.

3. **Car Charger:**
   - Use a car charger adapter to charge Baofeng radio batteries while on the go.
   - Plug the car charger adapter into the vehicle's power outlet and connect the charging cable to the radio.

4. **USB Charging:**
   - Some Baofeng radios support USB charging, allowing users to charge the battery using a USB cable connected to a computer or USB power adapter.
   - Ensure the USB power source provides sufficient voltage and current for charging the battery safely.

Battery Management:

1. **Regular Charging:**
   - Charge the Baofeng radio battery after each use to ensure it is fully charged and ready for the next operation.
   - Avoid leaving the battery discharged for extended periods, as this can lead to capacity loss and performance degradation.

2. **Avoiding Overcharging:**
   - Remove the battery from the charger once it is fully charged to prevent overcharging and minimize stress on the battery.

3. **Storing Batteries Properly:**
   - Store spare batteries in a cool, dry place away from direct sunlight and extreme temperatures.
   - Check the battery charge level periodically and recharge as needed to maintain optimal performance.

4. **Using Genuine Batteries:**
   - Use genuine Baofeng batteries or compatible batteries recommended by the manufacturer to ensure compatibility and reliability.
   - Avoid using counterfeit or low-quality batteries, as they may not provide adequate power or could damage the radio.

Effective battery management and charging practices are essential for maintaining the performance and longevity of Baofeng radios. By following proper battery management techniques and using appropriate charging methods, users can ensure reliable operation, prolong battery lifespan, and avoid downtime due to battery-related issues. Regular inspection, charging, and storage of batteries according to manufacturer recommendations are key to maximizing the lifespan and performance of Baofeng radio batteries.

Chapter Eight

Best Practices for Effective Communication with Baofeng Radio

Effective communication with Baofeng radios requires adherence to best practices to ensure clarity, reliability, and efficiency in transmitting and receiving messages. By following these practices, users can optimize their communication experience and maximize the capabilities of their radios.

Comprehensive List of Best Practices:

1. Clear and Concise Communication
2. Familiarize Yourself with Radio Etiquette
3. Use Proper Radio Procedures
4. Select Appropriate Channels and Frequencies
5. Monitor Channels for Activity
6. Maintain Good Radio Discipline

7. Adjust Squelch and Volume Settings
8. Use Headsets or External Microphones
9. Be Mindful of Battery Life
10.   Practice Situational Awareness

Clear and Concise Communication: Transmit messages in a clear, concise manner to ensure they are easily understood by recipients.

- Instead of saying, "I think I saw something," say, "I spotted a vehicle approaching from the east."

Familiarize Yourself with Radio Etiquette: Understand and follow established radio etiquette guidelines to maintain professionalism and respect on the airwaves.

- Use "over" to indicate the end of your transmission and signal that you are awaiting a response.

Use Proper Radio Procedures: Follow proper radio procedures for initiating and terminating communication, as well as acknowledging receipt of messages.

- Use "this is" or "from" to identify yourself when initiating communication, followed by your call sign or identifier.

Select Appropriate Channels and Frequencies: Choose channels and frequencies that are appropriate for your intended communication purpose and geographical location.

101

- Use a repeater frequency when communicating over long distances or in areas with obstructions.

Monitor Channels for Activity: Monitor channels for activity before transmitting to avoid interrupting ongoing conversations or emergency communications.

- Listen for a few moments to ensure the channel is clear before transmitting your message.

Maintain Good Radio Discipline: Exercise discipline in radio use by avoiding unnecessary transmissions, maintaining order on the airwaves, and adhering to established protocols.

- Refrain from transmitting jokes or irrelevant information that may clutter the channel.

Adjust Squelch and Volume Settings: Adjust squelch and volume settings as needed to optimize reception and minimize background noise.

- Increase squelch level to filter out weak signals or interference, or adjust volume for comfortable listening.

Use Headsets or External Microphones: Use headsets or external microphones to improve audio quality, reduce background noise, and enhance privacy during communication.

- Use a headset with a boom microphone for hands-free communication while on the move.

Be Mindful of Battery Life: Monitor battery levels and conserve power by turning off unnecessary features or reducing transmission time.

- Turn off backlight or keypad tones to extend battery life, or carry spare batteries for longer operations.

1**Practice Situational Awareness:** Maintain situational awareness of your surroundings and communication environment to adapt your communication strategy accordingly.

- Be aware of weather conditions, terrain features, and potential obstacles that may affect radio signal propagation or communication effectiveness.

Ways to Implement Best Practices:

1. **Training and Education:** Attend radio communication courses or training sessions to learn proper radio procedures and etiquette.

2. **Practice and Simulation:** Participate in simulated communication exercises or drills to practice implementing best practices in various scenarios.

3. **Continuous Improvement:** Regularly review and update your communication skills and techniques to adapt to changing environments and technology.

4. **Peer Feedback:** Seek feedback from experienced radio operators or peers to identify areas for improvement and refine your communication skills.

Effective communication with Baofeng radios requires adherence to best practices to ensure clarity, reliability, and efficiency in transmitting and receiving messages. By following these practices and continuously refining your communication skills, you can optimize your communication experience, maximize the capabilities of your radio, and contribute to a safe and efficient communication environment on the airwaves.

Radio Etiquette and Protocol: Enhancing Communication Effectiveness

Radio etiquette and protocol encompass a set of guidelines and procedures designed to promote clear, efficient, and respectful communication on the airwaves. By adhering to these standards, radio operators can minimize confusion, avoid misunderstandings, and maintain professionalism in their interactions. Let's delve into the intricacies of radio etiquette and protocol, exploring their definitions, key principles, and practical applications.

A Radio Etiquettes are set of unwritten rules and customs governing courteous behavior and communication practices among radio users.

Protocols on the other hand are established procedures and guidelines for conducting communication in a structured and efficient manner, often specific to a particular context or technology.

Common Radio Etiquette and Protocol:

1. Identify Yourself Clearly:
Before transmitting, clearly identify yourself and your call sign to ensure recipients know who is speaking.
- Example: "This is Alpha-1, over."

2. Listen Before Transmitting:
Listen to the channel for ongoing transmissions before transmitting to avoid interrupting ongoing conversations.
- Example: Listen for a few seconds before transmitting to ensure the channel is clear.

3. Use Standardized Phrases:

Use standardized phrases and terminology to convey messages clearly and efficiently.

- Example: "Roger" for acknowledgment, "Wilco" for acknowledgment and compliance.

4. Speak Clearly and Slowly:

Speak clearly and at a moderate pace to ensure your message is understood by recipien

- Example: "This is Bravo-2, requesting permission to land, over."

5. Avoid Jargon and Slang:

Avoid using jargon, slang, or abbreviations that may not be understood by all listeners.

- Example: Use "over" to indicate the end of your transmission, instead of "over and out."

6. Wait for Response:

After transmitting a message, wait for a response before transmitting again to allow recipients time to acknowledge or reply.

- Example: "This is Charlie-3, awaiting instructions, over."

7. Be Brief and Concise:

Keep transmissions brief and to the point to minimize airtime and convey information efficiently.

- Example: "This is Delta-4, requesting status update, over."

8. Acknowledge Receipt:

Acknowledge receipt of messages or instructions to confirm understanding and signal compliance.

- Example: "Received, out."

9. Respect Priority Traffic:

Yield to priority traffic, such as emergency communications or official transmissions, to ensure timely and appropriate response.

- Example: "Standby for priority traffic."

10. Maintain Professionalism:

Maintain professionalism and courtesy in all communications, refraining from engaging in arguments or disputes on the airwaves.

- Example: Address others respectfully and refrain from using offensive language or derogatory remarks.

Practical Application:

Let's consider some practical applications:

1. Scenario: Requesting Clearance to Takeoff
   - Proper Protocol: "Tower, this is Echo-5 requesting clearance for takeoff, over."
   - Etiquette: Wait for tower response before proceeding with takeoff.

2. Scenario: Reporting Weather Conditions

- Proper Protocol: "This is Foxtrot-6 reporting current weather conditions as follows, over."
- Etiquette: Provide concise and relevant weather information without unnecessary elaboration.

3. Scenario: Emergency Communication
- Proper Protocol: "Mayday, mayday, mayday! This is Golf-7, experiencing engine failure, over."
- Etiquette: Remain calm and provide relevant details to facilitate assistance.

Radio etiquette and protocol serve as essential guidelines for fostering effective, efficient, and respectful communication on the airwaves. By understanding and adhering to these standards, radio operators can enhance communication clarity, minimize errors, and contribute to a positive communication environment. Practicing proper etiquette and protocol not only improves communication effectiveness but also ensures safety and professionalism in radio operations.

Range Optimization Techniques in Baofeng Radio

Range optimization techniques in Baofeng radios are strategies aimed at maximizing the transmission and reception distances, ensuring reliable communication over longer distances. By implementing these techniques, users can improve the performance of their Baofeng radios and overcome obstacles that may limit their range. Here are some effective range optimization techniques for Baofeng radios:

1. **Use Quality Antennas:**

Replace the stock antenna with a higher quality antenna designed for better performance. A longer or more efficient antenna can significantly improve signal transmission and reception range.

2. **Select the Right Frequency:**

Choose frequencies that are optimal for the intended communication distance and environment. Lower frequencies typically travel farther, especially in outdoor settings, while higher frequencies may perform better in urban environments.

3. **Utilize Repeaters:**

Access repeater networks to extend the range of Baofeng radios. Repeaters receive signals on one frequency and retransmit them on another, effectively boosting the range of communication.

4. **Elevate Antennas:**

Position antennas at higher elevations to improve line-of-sight communication and minimize obstructions. Mounting antennas on tall buildings, hills, or towers can enhance signal propagation over longer distances.

5. **Adjust Power Levels:**

Increase the transmit power output of the radio, if possible, to maximize signal strength. However, be mindful of legal limitations and battery consumption associated with higher power levels.

6. **Optimize Antenna Orientation:**

Adjust the orientation of the antenna for optimal signal transmission. Experiment with vertical and horizontal orientations to find the position that provides the best signal strength.

7. **Reduce Interference:**

Minimize sources of interference that may disrupt communication signals. Avoid transmitting near power lines, electronic devices, or other radio frequency (RF) sources that could cause interference.

8. **Improve Grounding:**

Ensure proper grounding of antennas and radio equipment to minimize signal losses and improve overall performance. A well-grounded system can enhance signal propagation and reduce noise.

9. Use External Accessories:

Employ external accessories such as amplifiers, signal boosters, or directional antennas to enhance signal strength and extend communication range in challenging environments.

10. Practice Clear Line-of-Sight Communication:

Whenever possible, establish clear line-of-sight communication paths between transmitting and receiving stations to minimize signal attenuation and maximize range.

11. Perform Regular Maintenance:

Keep the radio and antenna clean and well-maintained to ensure optimal performance. Check for loose connections, damaged cables, or corroded components that may affect signal quality.

12. Utilize Radio Programming:

Program the radio with the most efficient channel settings, including proper bandwidth, modulation, and squelch settings, to optimize performance for specific communication scenarios.

By implementing these range optimization techniques, users can enhance the performance and reliability of their Baofeng radios, ensuring clear and effective communication over longer distances. Experimenting with different strategies and configurations can help users find the optimal settings for their specific communication needs and operating environments.

Group Communication Strategies

Group communication strategies are essential for facilitating effective and coordinated communication among multiple users using Baofeng radios. Whether for team coordination during outdoor activities, emergency response situations, or group events, implementing these strategies can enhance communication efficiency and ensure clarity and coherence in message transmission.

Establish Clear Communication Protocols:

- Define clear communication protocols outlining procedures for initiating, responding to, and concluding transmissions within the group.

- Designate a group leader responsible for coordinating communication and establishing communication protocols. For example, using phrases like "Alpha Team to Bravo Team, over" to initiate communication and "Bravo Team receiving, over" to acknowledge receipt.

Assign Roles and Responsibilities:

- Assign specific roles and responsibilities to group members to streamline communication and ensure efficient task execution.

- Designate a navigator responsible for providing location updates, a leader responsible for making decisions, and a communicator responsible for relaying messages between group members.

Use Clear and Concise Language:

Communicate using clear, concise language to convey information accurately and efficiently, avoiding ambiguity or confusion.

- For example, Instead of saying, "We need assistance," specify the nature of the assistance required, such as "Requesting medical assistance for injured hikers, over."

Implement Check-In and Check-Out Procedures:

Establish check-in and check-out procedures for group members to confirm their presence and departure, ensuring accountability and safety.

- Before embarking on an outdoor excursion, each group member checks in by radio, providing their name and status. Upon completion of the activity, they check out to confirm their safe return.

5. **Use Identifiers and Call Signs:**

Assign unique identifiers or call signs to group members to facilitate quick and accurate identification during communication.

- For example, Each group member adopts a call sign based on their role or position within the group, such as "Alpha Leader," "Bravo Medic," or "Charlie Navigator."

Establish Communication Protocols for Emergencies:

- Define communication protocols specific to emergency situations, outlining procedures for initiating emergency calls, providing location information, and requesting assistance.

- Designate a specific emergency channel or frequency for emergency communications, and establish predefined emergency codes or signals to indicate the severity of the situation.

Conduct Regular Communication Checks: Conduct regular communication checks to ensure all group members can hear and be heard, identify any communication issues, and make necessary adjustments.

- For example: Periodically conduct radio checks where each group member confirms their radio is functioning properly and can communicate with others.

Foster Active Listening: Encourage active listening among group members to ensure they fully understand messages received and can respond appropriately.

- Train group members to listen attentively to incoming transmissions, repeat key information for confirmation, and ask for clarification if needed.

Establish Communication Hierarchies: Establish clear communication hierarchies to streamline decision-making processes and ensure effective information flow within the group.

- Designate a chain of command outlining who communicates with whom and in what order, ensuring efficient dissemination of information.

Practice Coordination and Collaboration: Encourage coordination and collaboration among group members to share information, resources, and expertise, fostering a cohesive and unified team.

- Encourage group members to communicate openly, share updates, and collaborate on decision-making processes to achieve common goals.

By implementing these group communication strategies and practices, users can enhance coordination, collaboration, and effectiveness in communication using Baofeng radios, ensuring seamless interaction and achieving collective objectives with efficiency and clarity. Regular training, drills, and simulations can help reinforce these strategies and improve group communication proficiency over time.

Chapter Nine:

Real-Life Scenarios and Case Studies

Real-life scenarios and case studies provide practical examples of how Baofeng radios are used in various contexts, offering insights into communication challenges, strategies, and best practices. By examining these scenarios, users can gain a deeper understanding of how to effectively utilize Baofeng radios in real-world situations. Let's explore this chapter in detail, discussing what real-life scenarios and case studies are and providing a comprehensive list with explanations and examples:

What Are Real-Life Scenarios and Case Studies?

Real-life scenarios and case studies depict situations or events where Baofeng radios are utilized for communication purposes. These scenarios are based on actual experiences or hypothetical situations drawn from different industries, environments, and activities. Case studies provide detailed accounts of how Baofeng radios were employed to address communication challenges, solve problems, and achieve communication objectives in diverse settings.

Comprehensive List of Real-Life Scenarios and Case Studies:

1. Outdoor Recreation: Hiking Expedition
A group of hikers encounters communication challenges in a remote wilderness area.

- Limited line-of-sight communication due to rugged terrain and dense vegetation. Baofeng radios with extended range antennas and repeaters are used to maintain communication between hiking groups and base camp.

2. Emergency Response: Natural Disaster
Emergency responders face communication disruptions during a natural disaster.

- Disrupted communication infrastructure and limited access to traditional channels. Baofeng radios with pre-programmed emergency frequencies are deployed, and communication relay points are established to coordinate rescue efforts.

3. Construction Site Coordination:
Construction workers coordinate activities on a busy job site.

- Noisy environment with potential signal interference from heavy machinery. Baofeng radios with noise-canceling headsets are used, and frequencies are adjusted to minimize interference. Clear communication protocols are established for coordinating tasks and ensuring safety.

4. **Community Events: Festival Management:** Organizers manage communication at a large-scale community event.

- Multiple teams and departments coordinate activities across the event venue. Baofeng radios with designated channels for security, medical, and operations teams are used to facilitate communication. Regular check-ins and updates are conducted to ensure smooth event operations.

5. **Search and Rescue Mission:** Search and rescue teams respond to a missing person report in a remote area.

- Limited visibility and challenging terrain hamper communication efforts. Baofeng radios equipped with GPS and emergency signaling features are used to coordinate search efforts and communicate with command centers. Effective communication protocols are established to ensure efficient coordination and response.

6. **Outdoor Sports: Off-Road Adventure**
Off-road enthusiasts navigate challenging terrain in a remote wilderness area.

- Group members encounter communication difficulties due to distance and rugged terrain. Baofeng radios with long-range capabilities are used to maintain contact between vehicles and coordinate navigation. Emergency communication procedures are established in case of vehicle breakdowns or accidents.

Real-life scenarios and case studies offer practical examples of how Baofeng radios are utilized in various contexts, providing valuable insights into communication challenges, strategies, and best practices. By examining these scenarios and analyzing the solutions implemented, users can enhance their understanding of effective communication techniques and improve their ability to utilize Baofeng radios in real-world situations. Regular exposure to diverse case studies fosters learning, innovation, and continuous improvement in communication practices using Baofeng radios.

Chapter Ten:

Baofeng Official Resources

Baofeng official resources refer to the various tools, materials, and platforms provided by Baofeng for users to access information, support, and updates related to their radios. These resources play a crucial role in enhancing user experience, troubleshooting issues, and staying informed about the latest developments. Let's explore this chapter in detail, discussing what Baofeng official resources are and providing a comprehensive list with explanations and examples:

Baofeng official resources encompass a range of tools, materials, and platforms created and maintained by Baofeng to support users of their radios. These resources are designed to provide information, assistance, and updates related to radio operation, programming, troubleshooting, and more. By accessing Baofeng official resources, users can find answers to their questions, access technical support, and stay updated on product developments and announcements.

Baofeng Official Resources Includes:

1. **Baofeng Website:**

Baofeng's official website serves as a central hub for product information, user manuals, firmware updates, and support resources. Users can visit the Baofeng website to download user manuals, access firmware updates, and find answers to frequently asked questions (FAQs).

2. Online Support Portal:

Baofeng's online support portal provides technical support, troubleshooting guides, and customer service assistance. Here, users can submit support tickets, browse knowledge base articles, and engage with Baofeng support staff to resolve issues or seek guidance.

3. Official Documentation:

Baofeng provides official documentation, including user manuals, programming guides, and specification sheets, to assist users in operating and programming their radios. Users can download PDF versions of user manuals or programming guides from the Baofeng website for reference.

4. Firmware Update Center:

Baofeng offers a firmware update center where users can download the latest firmware updates for their radios to access new features, improvements, and bug fixes. Users can check for firmware updates on the Baofeng website and download the firmware files to update their radios using programming software.

5. Social Media Channels:

Baofeng maintains official social media channels, including Facebook, Twitter, and YouTube, to share product announcements, tutorials, and user stories. Users can follow Baofeng's social media channels to stay informed about new products, firmware updates, and instructional videos.

6. Online Forums and Communities:

Baofeng users often participate in online forums and communities dedicated to radio communication, where they can exchange information, share experiences, and seek advice from fellow enthusiasts. Users can join forums such as Reddit's r/Baofeng or specialized radio communication forums to engage with other users, ask questions, and learn from their experiences.

7. Official Distributors and Retailers:

Baofeng partners with official distributors and retailers worldwide to provide sales support, product information, and customer service. Users can contact authorized Baofeng distributors or retailers for assistance with product purchases, warranty claims, or technical support.

8. Email Newsletter Subscriptions:
Baofeng offers email newsletter subscriptions to users interested in receiving updates, promotions, and announcements directly to their inbox. Users can sign up for Baofeng's newsletter on the

official website to stay informed about new products, firmware updates, and special offers.

Baofeng official resources encompass a range of tools, materials, and platforms provided by Baofeng to support users of their radios. From the official website and online support portal to social media channels and online forums, these resources offer valuable information, assistance, and updates to help users operate, program, troubleshoot, and stay informed about Baofeng radios. By accessing Baofeng official resources, users can enhance their user experience, resolve issues, and stay up-to-date on the latest developments in radio communication technology.

Recommended Accessories for Baofeng Radios

Recommended accessories for Baofeng radios are additional tools, attachments, or peripherals that enhance the functionality, performance, and usability of Baofeng handheld transceivers. These accessories are designed to complement the capabilities of Baofeng radios and provide users with added convenience, versatility, and customization options. Let's explore this topic in detail, discussing what recommended accessories are and providing a comprehensive list with explanations and examples

Recommended accessories for Baofeng radios are optional add-ons or enhancements that users can purchase separately to augment their radio experience. These accessories are designed to address specific needs, preferences, or usage scenarios and may include items such as antennas, batteries, chargers, cases, earpieces, programming cables, and more. By investing in recommended accessories, users can customize their Baofeng radios to better suit their communication requirements and preferences.

Recommended Accessories:

1. High-Gain Antennas:
High-gain antennas enhance signal reception and transmission range, allowing users to communicate over longer distances or in challenging environments.
   - Example: Nagoya NA-771 or Diamond SRH805S antennas are popular options for improving the performance of Baofeng radios.

2. Extended Capacity Batteries:

Extended capacity batteries provide longer operating times between charges, ideal for users who require extended communication durations. Baofeng BL-5L or BL-8 batteries offer higher capacity than standard batteries and are compatible with various Baofeng radio models.

3. **Desktop Chargers:**

Desktop chargers allow users to conveniently charge multiple radio batteries simultaneously, without needing to connect each radio to a separate charger. Baofeng original desktop chargers or third-party multi-bay chargers provide efficient charging solutions for Baofeng radio batteries.

4. **Car Chargers:**

Car chargers enable users to charge Baofeng radio batteries while on the go, using the vehicle's power outlet. Baofeng car chargers with cigarette lighter adapters provide convenient charging options for users who frequently travel by car.

5. **Carrying Cases and Holsters:**

Carrying cases and holsters protect Baofeng radios from damage, dust, and debris, while providing convenient storage and portability. Nylon or leather carrying cases with belt clips or shoulder straps offer protection and easy access to Baofeng radios during outdoor activities or fieldwork.

6. **Earpieces and Headsets:**

Earpieces and headsets allow users to listen and transmit messages discreetly, hands-free, and with improved audio clarity. Surveillance-style earpieces with built-in microphones or noise-canceling headsets enhance communication privacy and effectiveness in noisy environments.

7. **Programming Cables and Software:**

Programming cables and software enable users to program Baofeng radios with custom frequencies, channels, and settings, facilitating advanced configuration and optimization. Baofeng USB programming cables and compatible programming software such as CHIRP for Baofeng's official programming software allow users to customize their radios to meet specific communication needs.

8. **External Microphones and Speakers:**

External microphones and speakers enhance audio quality and intelligibility during communication, particularly in noisy or windy conditions. Baofeng-compatible external microphones with clip-on lapel mics or external speakers with amplification capabilities improve communication effectiveness in various environments.

9. **Waterproof Bags and Cases:**

Waterproof bags and cases provide protection for Baofeng radios against water, moisture, and environmental elements, ensuring durability and reliability in outdoor or wet conditions. Waterproof pouches or cases with sealed closures and transparent windows allow users to operate Baofeng radios while providing protection from rain, splashes, or submersion.

10. Carrying Straps and Lanyards:

Carrying straps and lanyards offer added security and comfort when carrying Baofeng radios, preventing accidental drops or loss. Adjustable nylon straps or paracord lanyards with quick-release buckles provide convenient carrying options for handheld Baofeng radios during outdoor activities or fieldwork.

Recommended accessories for Baofeng radios offer users additional functionality, versatility, and convenience to enhance their radio communication experience. Whether extending range with high-gain antennas, improving audio clarity with earpieces, or customizing settings with programming cables, users can personalize their Baofeng radios to meet their specific needs and preferences. By investing in recommended accessories, users can maximize the performance, usability, and enjoyment of their Baofeng radios in various communication scenarios and environments.

Glossary of Terms for Baofeng Radios

This glossary of terms for Baofeng radios provides definitions, explanations, and clarifications of key terms, acronyms, and technical terminology commonly used in the context of Baofeng handheld transceivers. This glossary serves as a valuable tool for users to understand and familiarize themselves with the terminology associated with Baofeng radios, enabling clearer communication, troubleshooting, and operation. Let's explore this topic in detail, discussing what a glossary of terms is and providing a comprehensive list with explanations and examples:

A glossary of terms for Baofeng radios is a curated list of terms and definitions relevant to the operation, features, components, and technical aspects of Baofeng handheld transceivers. It serves as a reference guide for users to quickly look up and understand unfamiliar terminology encountered while using Baofeng radios. The glossary aims to clarify complex concepts, abbreviations, and industry-specific jargon, facilitating effective communication and comprehension among users.

Glossary Terms:

1. Frequency:
The rate at which a radio signal oscillates, measured in Hertz (Hz), kilohertz (kHz), megahertz (MHz), or gigahertz (GHz).

- Example: The FM radio band operates in the frequency range of 88 MHz to 108 MHz.

2. Channel:

A predetermined frequency or combination of frequencies used for communication between radios.

- Example: Channel 1 may be programmed to transmit and receive on a frequency of 462.5625 MHz.

3. Squelch:
A circuit that mutes the audio output of a radio when no signal is present, preventing background noise from being heard.

- Example: Adjusting the squelch level on a Baofeng radio eliminates static noise when no incoming signal is detected.

4. CTCSS (Continuous Tone-Coded Squelch System):
A method of filtering out unwanted radio transmissions by using sub-audible tones to selectively open the squelch only for signals with the correct tone.

- Example: Baofeng radios can be programmed with specific CTCSS tones to access or filter out transmissions on designated channels.

5. DCS (Digital-Coded Squelch):
A digital squelch system that uses encoded digital signals to selectively open the squelch on compatible radios.

- Example: Baofeng radios equipped with DCS capabilities can communicate with other radios using compatible DCS codes for added privacy and security.

6. **VOX (Voice-Operated Transmission):**

A feature that enables hands-free operation of a radio by automatically transmitting when the user speaks into the microphone.

- Example: Baofeng radios with VOX functionality allow users to activate transmission by voice command without pressing the Push-To-Talk (PTT) button.

7. **PTT (Push-To-Talk):**

A button or switch on a radio that, when pressed, activates transmission and allows the user to speak into the microphone.

- Example: Pressing the PTT button on a Baofeng radio initiates transmission, allowing the user to communicate with other radios on the same channel.

8. **Repeater**:

A radio station that receives signals on one frequency and retransmits them on another frequency to extend the range of communication.

- Example: Baofeng radios can access repeaters to communicate over longer distances or in areas with obstructed line-of-sight.

9. **Scan**:
A function that automatically searches and monitors multiple channels or frequencies for activity, allowing users to listen for incoming transmissions.
- Example: Baofeng radios can be set to scan a range of frequencies to detect and monitor active channels.

10. **Programming:**
The process of configuring a radio's settings, channels, frequencies, and features using programming software or manual input.

- Example: Programming a Baofeng radio involves entering desired frequencies, assigning channels, setting squelch levels, and configuring other parameters for optimal performance.

A glossary of terms for Baofeng radios provides users with a comprehensive reference guide to understand and interpret the terminology associated with handheld transceivers. By familiarizing themselves with key terms, definitions, and concepts, users can effectively communicate, troubleshoot, and operate Baofeng radios with confidence and clarity. The glossary enhances users' understanding of radio technology, features, and functions, empowering them to make informed decisions and optimize their radio communication experience.

Conclusion

In conclusion, the "Baofeng Radio User's Guide" serves as an indispensable companion for anyone looking to maximize their experience with Baofeng handheld transceivers. Throughout this guide, we have explored the ins and outs of Baofeng radios, from understanding their basic functions to mastering advanced features and troubleshooting common issues.

By delving into topics such as initial setup and configuration, programming, recommended accessories, and real-life scenarios, users gain a comprehensive understanding of how to harness the full potential of their Baofeng radios. Whether you're a novice seeking to grasp the fundamentals or a seasoned operator looking to fine-tune your skills, this guide equips you with the knowledge and resources needed to excel in radio communication.

As technology continues to evolve and new challenges arise, it is essential to stay informed and adaptable. Baofeng radios offer versatility, reliability, and affordability, making them invaluable tools in various settings, including emergency response, outdoor recreation, construction, and more. With the information provided in this guide, users can confidently navigate the world of radio communication and unlock endless possibilities with their Baofeng radios.

Remember, communication is key, and Baofeng radios empower you to connect, collaborate, and stay informed wherever your adventures take you. Whether you're exploring the great outdoors, coordinating events, or responding to emergencies, let your Baofeng radio be your trusted companion in staying connected with the world around you.

Thank you for embarking on this journey with us. May your experiences with Baofeng radios be fulfilling, enriching, and above all, enjoyable.

Happy communicating!

www.ingramcontent.com/pod-product-compliance
Lightning Source LLC
LaVergne TN
LVHW081529050326
832903LV00025B/1696